New Harbinger Journals for Change

Research shows that journaling has a universally positive effect on mental health. But in the midst of life's difficulties—such as stress, anxiety, depression, relationship problems, parenting challenges, or even obsessive or negative thoughts—where do you begin? New Harbinger *Journals for Change* combine evidence-based psychology with proven-effective guided journaling techniques to help you make lasting personal change—one page at a time. Written by renowned mental health and wellness experts, *Journals for Change* provide a creative and safe space to process difficult emotions, work through challenges, reflect on what matters, and set intentions for the future.

Since 1973, New Harbinger has published practical, user-friendly self-help books and workbooks to help readers make positive change. Our *Journals for Change* offer the same powerfully effective tools—without ever *feeling* like therapy. If you're committed to improving your mental health, these easy-to-use guided journals can help you take small, actionable steps toward lasting well-being.

For a complete list of journals in our *Journals for Change* series, visit newharbinger.com.

"Melanie Greenberg's scientific approach to managing stress is much needed in our modern world. By breaking down this science into actionable exercises, her workbook makes these skills even easier to digest and use in real life. For anyone who is struggling with stress, *The Stress-Proof Brain Guided Journal* is a great resource!"

—**Tchiki Davis**, founder of The Berkeley Well-Being Institute

"Melanie Greenberg's *The Stress-Proof Brain Guided Journal* is a game changer. Blending neuroscience and practical exercises, she offers a transformative road map to calm and resilience. For anyone seeking to navigate life's challenges with grace, this journal is your compass!"

—**Elisha Goldstein, PhD**, author of *Uncovering Happiness,* and coauthor of *A Mindfulness-Based Stress Reduction Workbook*

"A great resource for those looking to decrease stress and anxiety through practical take-home skills. Many of my clients struggle with childhood or relationship traumas that often get in the way of their healing. This book provides a trauma-informed approach to observing, reflecting on, and changing some of the anxious patterns that creep up. I recommend it to those looking for a guide to help!"

—**Kaytee Gillis, LCSW-BACS**, psychotherapist; specialist in relational trauma; and author of three books, including *Breaking the Cycle*

"Through brilliantly curated writing exercises on everything from taming negative self-talk to surfing your emotions, Melanie Greenberg puts the tools for stress-proofing in your hands. Follow her lead to train your brain with the rock-solid mental muscle needed to not only survive, but thrive!"

—**Albert Wong, PhD**, director of the trauma certificate program at Somatopia

"Melanie Greenberg offers a comprehensive and invaluable resource for readers seeking relief from stress. With brilliantly structured journal prompts, readers learn how to rewire the brain's natural negative bias to feel happier and cope better. She translates complex neuropsychology concepts into bite-sized, actionable remedies helpful to anyone seeking lasting relief from worry and stress. This book is a remarkable and much-needed prescription for mental health and well-being."

—**Gina Simmons Schneider, PhD**, psychotherapist, executive coach, and author of *Frazzlebrain*

"*The Stress-Proof Brain Guided Journal* expertly pinpoints your stressors—be they from day-to-day life, at work, from a lingering trauma, or in your relationships. Insightful, personalized steps teach you how to alter *your* emotional response to individual stressors and guide you to a calmer, more resilient, happier you. It's a win-win guide for anyone who wants to build their brain power and be able to manage their stress and anxiety. Who doesn't want to do that?"

—**Susan Newman, PhD**, social psychologist, and author of *The Book of No*

"*The Stress-Proof Brain Guided Journal* is a brilliant fusion of neuroscience research and practical self-help. This book expertly guides readers through transformative writing exercises, offering a clear path to rewiring emotional responses to stress. Backed by neuroscience insights, it empowers individuals to cultivate resilience and lasting calm. A must-read for anyone seeking a science-backed, hands-on approach to managing stress and achieving emotional well-being."

—**Tara Well, PhD**, associate professor of psychology at Barnard College, and author of *Mirror Meditation*

The Stress-Proof Brain

GUIDED JOURNAL

Writing Practices to Rewire Your Emotional Response to Stress & Feel Calm

MELANIE GREENBERG, PhD

New Harbinger Publications, Inc.

Publisher's Note

This publication is designed to provide accurate and authoritative information in regard to the subject matter covered. It is sold with the understanding that the publisher is not engaged in rendering psychological, financial, legal, or other professional services. If expert assistance or counseling is needed, the services of a competent professional should be sought.

NEW HARBINGER PUBLICATIONS is a registered trademark of New Harbinger Publications, Inc.

New Harbinger Publications is an employee-owned company.

New Harbinger Publications, Inc.
5720 Shattuck Avenue
Oakland, CA 94609
www.newharbinger.com

Cover design by Sara Christian

Interior design by Sara Christian

Acquired by Jess O'Brien

Edited by Karen Schader

Printed in the United States of America

26 25 24

10 9 8 7 6 5 4 3 2 1 First Printing

Contents

Engaging the Cortex to Stop the Stress Cycle

You Can Change Your Brain to Stress Less

Hello, friend. Welcome.

You are stressed. Your stress may be due to an unexpected event, a life transition, or unending daily hassles that create new demands and uncertainty. Or all the above! Whatever its source, you know the feeling of being stressed out: You feel thrown off balance. Your thoughts race at breakneck speed as you imagine negative consequences or try to come up with quick solutions. Your heart pounds, and your breathing gets shallow as waves of fear emanate from your chest and belly. Your muscles tighten. You feel as if you can't sit still or think straight. You're exhausted and worried. You may criticize yourself and regret having gotten into a stressful situation.

Eventually, this uncomfortable feeling becomes too much, and you may numb yourself with food, alcohol, or mindless TV. Or you may drive yourself so hard that you get worn out, become cranky, and find yourself living an unbalanced, unhealthy life.

You may blame and criticize yourself for these unproductive responses to stress, but you shouldn't. Although you can't eliminate stress, you can do a lot to control it. You can overcome its debilitating effects that keep you from creating success in life, whether personal or professional. When you understand your brain's hardwired stress response, you can put your brain on a more calm, focused, and positive track. Handling your stress in this way will bring you more happiness and success.

This journal will help you build a stress-proof brain by transforming the way you react to stress. Its writing prompts are designed to deepen and personalize your understanding of stress in your life, step by step. It's designed to help you curb unhelpful responses, such as avoidance, persistent worrying, and fearful thinking; gain clarity and focus; restore your sense of control and a growth mindset; use grit and self-compassion to motivate yourself; and live a healthy and balanced life in the face of stress.

Like the companion book *The Stress-Proof Brain*, this journal is divided into three parts. In the first part, you'll closely examine your brain's and body's stress responses. You'll also learn what type of stressors you're facing and how stress affects your mental and physical health.

In the second part, you'll learn all about the amygdala, your brain's threat detector. You'll work on skills for facing difficult emotions, rather than avoiding them, and you'll learn ways to see your stressors as more controllable and use self-compassion to help your amygdala relax. Your journaling will focus on how to turn off the immediate alarm at the moment of distress.

In the final part, you'll work with the prefrontal cortex, your brain's CEO, by journaling to build your skills to combat worry, perfectionism, and hypervigilance. You'll learn to recruit your thinking brain to positive ends. You'll also learn how to view your stressors as challenges and focus on expanding your coping skills. The prompts in this section will teach you how to engage your prefrontal cortex for long-term neurological change. This is how you cement your gains and develop new neural pathways to guide your response to stress in a new, more intentional, values-based direction. At your journey's end, you can always revisit the most resonant prompts, deepening your understanding over time. That is the purpose of this journal: to provide you with brain-based coping skills that help you reorient your brain to be more resilient to stress.

Each entry has three parts: observe, reflect, and change. This structure allows you to dive deeper into the essence of the strategy you're exploring and make it part of your daily life. In some cases, the prompts encourage contemplation and lead to new insights. In other cases, they deepen your stress-response skills. Because expressing your own relationship to information helps deepen your understanding of it, the prompts ask you to write and reflect upon your personal experiences.

Although stress is a fact of life, you don't have to let it run your life. It doesn't have to overwhelm you or keep you stuck in ways of thinking and behaving that interfere with your health, happiness, and ability to meet your life goals. You can be the boss of your own brain, keeping your prefrontal cortex firmly in charge so that it can calm down your amygdala, making you less reactive to stress.

Understanding Your Stress

Measuring Your Level of Stress

To begin, take a moment to assess your perceived stress, or how stressed you feel, regardless of the reason why. Your feelings of being stressed and out of control are just as important as the actual stressors you face. This is good news, because you can't always choose what you have to deal with in life, but you can change how you feel and think about stress.

OBSERVE

For each statement below, circle the number that best represents your answer, where 0 = never, 1 = occasionally or almost never, 2 = sometimes, 3 = fairly often, and 4 = very often.

In the past month:

I have been upset because of an unexpected event or frustration.	0 1 2 3 4
I have believed that I couldn't control important life outcomes.	0 1 2 3 4
I have felt on edge and stressed out.	0 1 2 3 4
I have believed that things weren't going my way.	0 1 2 3 4
I have believed that I had more to handle than I could deal with.	0 1 2 3 4
I have felt irritable and impatient about small things.	0 1 2 3 4
I have felt my heart racing or butterflies in my stomach.	0 1 2 3 4
I have been unable to sleep because of my worries.	0 1 2 3 4
I have felt anxious when I woke up in the morning.	0 1 2 3 4
I have had difficulty concentrating because of my problems.	0 1 2 3 4

If you circled at least two 2s, 3s, or 4s, you're probably feeling at least moderately stressed. If you circled many 3s or 4s, you're probably under high stress and aren't managing it well on your own. (In that case, you may want to consult a mental health professional in addition to using the tools in this book.)

REFLECT

As you begin this journey, you'll want to identify what you hope to get out of it. Write about how stress is affecting your attitude, your mood, your relationships, your health, or your spirituality.

CHANGE

Reread the reflections you just wrote. Take a moment to imagine what your life would look like if you were more resilient to stress and had better coping skills. What would a less stressed life look like to you?

Major Life Events

Stress has many sources—daily hassles, trauma, fallout from negative childhood experiences, and more. Major life events are one source that affects most people. Among these events are developmental transitions—changes at particular stages of your life that require you to adapt to new circumstances. They can bring stress and anxiety, but they can also contribute to a sense of meaning in life and accomplishment.

OBSERVE

Have you experienced any of these transitions in the past year that were at least moderately stressful for you? Check them off.

- ☐ Moving house or buying a house
- ☐ Pregnancy or having a baby
- ☐ Adopting a child
- ☐ Kids leaving home
- ☐ Starting a new position or getting a promotion
- ☐ Starting college or graduate study, or transferring schools
- ☐ Getting engaged or married
- ☐ Retiring
- ☐ Graduating from college
- ☐ Something else (describe): ____________________

____

Some major life events can cause upheaval; stir up anger, fear, or sadness; and require you to devote time and money to coping with them. They often represent failure or obstacles to progress in an important life role. They may create fear and uncertainty, or conversely, they may challenge you to let go of certain dreams and change your path.

Check off all the events that occurred during the past year or that don't feel completely resolved for you.

- ☐ The death of a loved one or pet
- ☐ Getting fired from a job or experiencing unemployment (you or your partner)
- ☐ Academic failure
- ☐ Being turned down for a promotion, position, or program
- ☐ Being diagnosed with a serious or chronic health problem (you or a family member)
- ☐ A falling-out with a family member, coworker, supervisor, or close friend
- ☐ Your partner having a physical or emotional affair
- ☐ The breakup of a romantic relationship
- ☐ An unwanted pregnancy or abortion
- ☐ Infertility, miscarriage, or stillbirth
- ☐ An elderly family member needing care
- ☐ Serious financial or legal problems
- ☐ A car or bicycle accident or other injury
- ☐ Relocation
- ☐ Something else (describe): ____________________

____

REFLECT

Think of a major life event that you're currently dealing with and write about it. Try to identify the most stressful aspect of the event, and explain why it is or was so stressful.

CHANGE

Is there a way for you to accept this situation even if you didn't choose it? Can you work on accepting those parts of the situation that are out of your control? Explain.

If you feel inspired, repeat the reflect and change prompts for other major life events that are contributing to your current stress level.

Chronic Stressors

Chronic stressors are repeated or continuous stress-inducing situations in important areas of your life, like marriage, parenting, work, school, and family relationships. Work, while it can be a source of life satisfaction and self-esteem, is often a source of chronic stress. Loneliness is another common chronic stressor. Your brain is wired to connect with other people, because of the way our ancestors lived in groups and relied on one another, and it interprets loneliness as a stressor. Note that there are also two different kinds of loneliness. One comes from social isolation; the other is how lonely you feel: whether you feel cared about or that your needs are important to others.

OBSERVE

Check off all the stressors you experience on a regular basis.

- ☐ Fights with your partner, roommates, or neighbors
- ☐ Being rejected or let down by potential dating partners
- ☐ Financial stress; too much debt
- ☐ A partner, child, or parent with a mental or serious physical illness
- ☐ A partner, child, or parent who abuses substances
- ☐ Caring for a child, adult, or pet with serious illness or disability
- ☐ Academic or achievement difficulties
- ☐ Difficulty fulfilling responsibilities because of time, money, or health issues

- ☐ A lack of support or cooperation from others
- ☐ Negative interactions with friends, family, or coworkers
- ☐ A noisy, crowded, or uncomfortable living situation
- ☐ Chronic pain, disease, or disability
- ☐ Monotonous work, unreasonable demands, or not feeling valued for your contributions
- ☐ Excessive travel (for example, a long daily commute or weekly travel for work)
- ☐ Chronic dissatisfaction with your weight
- ☐ An eating disorder
- ☐ Dealing with a difficult ex-partner or blended-family situation
- ☐ Something else (describe): ______________________________

How stressful is your job? Check off all the stressors you experience on a regular basis.

- ☐ High demands for productivity or performance
- ☐ Insufficient time, equipment, or people to do the job
- ☐ Not enough authority or control over decisions
- ☐ Difficult, demanding, or manipulative people
- ☐ Having to be constantly "on" without a break
- ☐ A lack of meaning in your job or the company's mission
- ☐ Work interfering with family life
- ☐ Insufficient training or support to do your job
- ☐ A hostile or unreasonable boss
- ☐ A lack of appreciation or reward for your work

- ☐ A lack of support from coworkers
- ☐ Monotonous or boring work
- ☐ Job insecurity
- ☐ Not feeling fairly treated or compensated
- ☐ Feeling burned out or exhausted

Now, how lonely are you? Check off all the statements that are true for you.

- ☐ I don't have people to hang out with or do things with.
- ☐ When I need help, there's nobody to ask.
- ☐ I don't have close friends.
- ☐ I feel shut out or excluded.
- ☐ I don't feel part of a group or community.
- ☐ I don't have anyone to talk to.
- ☐ My relationships are superficial.
- ☐ I have a hard time making friends.
- ☐ I don't get invited anywhere.
- ☐ I feel alone most of the time.

REFLECT

Consider one of the items you checked. What do you feel when this happens? What have you done to try to deal with it in the past?

CHANGE

What might you do in the future to help you cope? For job-related stressors, would it help to speak up, delegate tasks, accept some limitations, or look for a different job? For stress related to loneliness, how could you be more in contact with friends and family, connect with your neighbors or colleagues, or find ways to be a caring, contributing member of your community? What are some steps you might take to begin learning and practicing these strategies?

If you feel inspired, repeat the reflect and change prompts for your other chronic stressors.

Daily Hassles

Daily hassles are the minor irritations we all experience: the printer jams or you lose your keys. You get stuck in traffic, or there's nothing to eat in the house. You get a parking ticket or have to pay late fees. Your partner is grumpy or your kids don't pick up their stuff. Your dog gets muddy or digs a hole in the yard.

These annoyances can constantly trigger your stress response at low levels, adding up to a lot of frustration and interfering with your goals. Although some people recover quickly from these types of stressors, others become sensitized and have a stronger reaction.

OBSERVE

What are some hassles you experience on a regular basis? Think about things like household chores, emails that need answering, costly or time-consuming home or car repairs, trouble with logistics related to childcare, the demands others make on your time, and other daily stressors.

REFLECT

How do your daily hassles drain your energy, make you more anxious, or complicate situations? How do they affect your life? For example, do they block you from important goals? Do they seem unnecessary or due to incompetence? Do they accumulate so you feel that you don't have enough time to recover from one by the time the next one happens?

CHANGE

What can you do to minimize daily hassles? Could making a conscious effort to focus on one thing at a time help? Is there anything you can delegate, outsource, or eliminate—perhaps by asking family or coworkers for help, hiring help, or talking to your boss about making a change at work? Or can you change your process or create a system—say, install a hook for keys, put your monthly bills on autopay, or start a new family routine where everyone spends five minutes after dinner putting things away?

Even if you're already experiencing the negative effects of stress, it's not too late to make a difference. Your brain and body have remarkable self-healing capacities.

Trauma's Effect on Stress Reactions

A trauma is an event that involves a threat—whether actual or perceived—to life, or physical or emotional harm to you or your loved ones. Many difficult childhood experiences can be traumatic, as can experiences like being in a serious accident, being assaulted, having a life-threatening illness, serving in military combat, or living through a natural disaster. Whatever its source, trauma can make you more psychologically and physiologically reactive to stress in the present. It can affect how you interpret the meaning of stressful events and how easily you get triggered into feeling helpless, unsafe, or incompetent.

This is heavy stuff. But it's important to understand and respect your own sensitivities when it comes to stress, so that you don't blame yourself for overreacting.

OBSERVE

Check off any of the following events you've been exposed to as an adult.

- ☐ Physical violence (toward you or a loved one)
- ☐ The death of a spouse, parent, child, or friend
- ☐ A verbally or emotionally abusive relationship
- ☐ A car accident in which someone was seriously injured or killed
- ☐ A natural disaster
- ☐ A serious or life-threatening illness, accident, or injury (your own or a loved one's)
- ☐ Robbery or burglary

- ☐ Being stalked or physically threatened
- ☐ Sexual assault or harassment
- ☐ Military combat
- ☐ Something shocking or gruesome (in real life)

Now check off any events you were exposed to prior to the age of eighteen.

- ☐ Parental separation or divorce
- ☐ A seriously ill or injured family member
- ☐ A family member with a mental health or substance use problem
- ☐ Witnessing family violence
- ☐ The death of a family member or close friend
- ☐ Physical abuse
- ☐ Sexual abuse
- ☐ Emotional abuse or a narcissistic parent
- ☐ Physical or emotional neglect
- ☐ Abandonment
- ☐ Being adopted
- ☐ Homelessness or poverty
- ☐ Being bullied (threats, humiliation, deliberate exclusion, and so on)

Mindfulness, facing and accepting your emotions, self-compassion, and understanding what aspects of the situation you can control can help you deal with the emotional aftereffects of trauma.

REFLECT

In what ways is trauma affecting how you respond to stress? As you're writing, see if you notice any behaviors or rules (such as "Don't ask for help" or "Don't show your feelings") that you developed as a result of past stressors or traumas and are using now. List them here.

CHANGE

Over the next few days, plan to do one thing—even a small one—to try to break one of the rules you wrote about. Once you've done it, come back to this journal and write about the experience. Was it hard? Did it ease your stress in some way, or give you a sense of accomplishment?

Seeing How Your Stressors Add Up

In the face of major life events, if you feel overwhelmed, emotionally flooded, unable to think clearly, or scared to act, this isn't your fault or a sign that something is wrong with you. As you've discovered, big life transitions can affect our mental health and make us more reactive. So can traumatic events, even from childhood. Even daily hassles can turn to major stress, because we have fewer resources to deal with the unexpected stuff. But once you know your stressors, you can learn skills that will give you a stress-proof brain. It starts by understanding how your stressors connect.

OBSERVE

Consider how all your stressors add up. Check in with yourself, and honestly observe how it feels to be dealing with all these issues at once. What comes to mind? Are some stressors affecting your reaction to others?

REFLECT

In what ways could your new clarity about what is stressing you out and your cumulative stressors help you understand your stress? How might you offer yourself some understanding and self-compassion for all that you're going through?

CHANGE

Think about a time when your resilience helped you overcome or achieve something. Recall how your focus and grit helped you overcome that challenge or meet that important personal goal. How can you apply those qualities to overcome your stress now? What inner resources and personal values can you lean on to overcome your stress?

You have to keep reminding yourself that it's not your fault you're sensitive to the things you're sensitive to, and that you can train your brain to become more resilient to stress.

Your Brain on Stress

Much of the human brain's physiological response to stress was laid down through thousands of years of evolution. A programmed stress response helped our ancestors take fast action to keep from being eaten by lions or failing to compete for food. In that sense, it was certainly a good thing!

Unfortunately, the same programmed response isn't too good at helping us deal with modern-day stressors. These situations don't generally call for physical action. They require understanding people's intentions; dealing with failure, loss, or uncertainty; solving logistical problems; or sustaining mental effort. And they require us to process lots of information in a short time, juggle competing priorities, and deal with a rapidly changing world.

If you're feeling stressed, it may be because your brain is oversensitive to danger. There are a few parts of your brain that shape your emotional and behavioral response to a stressful situation:

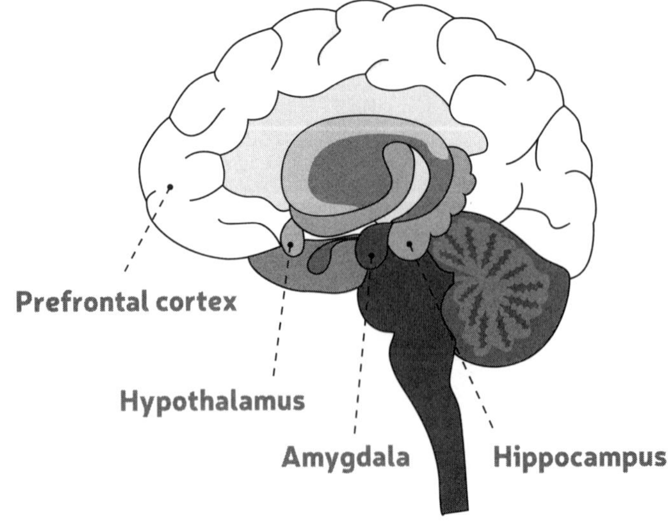

- ***Amygdala:*** Your brain's alarm center. It senses threats and other emotionally significant information and initiates the stress response.
- ***Hypothalamus:*** Your brain's operations manager. It coordinates the release of stress hormones to ready your body for fighting or fleeing.
- ***Hippocampus:*** Your brain's biographer. It stores and retrieves conscious memories about the current situation as well as previous stressors you've experienced, how you responded, and resulting outcomes. This allows you to learn from past experience and anticipate what's likely to happen.
- ***Prefrontal cortex:*** Your brain's CEO. It puts together information from your amygdala and hippocampus to create a planned, motivated response to stress. It communicates back and forth with the amygdala to modify your response as the stressor unfolds.

When your amygdala first notices a stressor, it signals your hypothalamus to initiate a lightning-fast chemical response, releasing the hormones adrenaline and norepinephrine into your bloodstream to ready your body to fight or flee. In these moments, you may notice your heart rate speeding up, your breathing getting quicker, increased alertness, and a general boost of energy.

This is an automatic process that is hard to grab control of, but control is possible. And recognizing it is the first step.

OBSERVE

Write about a specific stressful event or experience from the past as a first-person story (using words like "I" and "me"). Give as much detail as you can about what happened and what you did when you felt really stressed out.

REFLECT

Keep staying in the memory. How did your mind and body feel then? Write down as much as you can about your feelings and body sensations.

Now take a breath and check in with your body. How do you feel right now? Use a point or an asterisk to mark your feeling on this line.

RELAXED ———————————————— ON EDGE

CHANGE

Now you're going to rewrite your story. How would the ending be different if you recognized what your brain was doing in the moment? Imagine an alternative ending for when your brain gets super activated.

After writing an alternative ending, take a breath and check in with your body again. How do you feel right now? Use a point or an asterisk to mark your feeling on the line.

RELAXED ———————————————— ON EDGE

Fight, Flight, and Freeze

When you feel stressed, you likely feel fear or anger. These emotions are the result of your perception of the situation as a threat, sending you into fight-or-flight mode. Your brain reacts, summoning glucose for quick thinking, making your heart pump faster, and increasing blood flow to the muscles of your arms and legs to prepare your body for fighting or fleeing.

But sometimes fight or flight doesn't work. With some stressors, you can't get away or defend yourself. The only thing left to do is trying to numb yourself to the inevitable pain. And your body has a mechanism to do just that: a primitive "freeze" response that's carried throughout your body by your *vagus nerve*, which controls involuntary functions such as your heart rate and digestion. The freeze response isn't unique to humans; it occurs in many animal species. Think of the "deer in the headlights" effect.

Although part of your stress response is hardwired and automatic, you can change the way your brain processes and interprets stress. It's possible to transform feeling stressed into feeling challenged and energized or feeling grounded and self-confident.

OBSERVE

In what particular ways do your body and brain tend to become hijacked by stress? Do you typically experience a fight response? A flight response? A freeze response? Describe it.

REFLECT

Take some time to reflect and write what comes to mind now that you know your response to stress is hardwired and automatic. Does knowing that your reaction to stress is an evolutionary response change how you view your stress? In what way?

CHANGE

What are the automatic responses to stress that don't serve you well? What would it look like for you to have awareness and control of your reactions to stress in your day-to-day life? In your relationships? At work?

Stress and Your Nervous System

Once initiated by your amygdala, your stress response is distributed throughout your body by your *autonomic nervous system*, or ANS. The ANS, which consists of nerve cells in your brain and spinal cord, has two branches: your *sympathetic nervous system* and your *parasympathetic nervous system*.

Your sympathetic nervous system (SNS) acts as your ANS's accelerator. It communicates with your adrenal glands to stimulate the release of the hormones adrenaline and norepinephrine, which put your whole body on high alert and ready for action. When the danger is over, your parasympathetic nervous system (PNS) acts as a brake, calming down your system and facilitating a return to a resting state and continuation of non-emergency functions, such as sleepiness, appetite, and sex drive (the fun stuff!).

When these two systems and their functions are in balance, you're in what's known as *homeostasis*. But if stress is excessive or too prolonged, your ANS can become inflexible—your PNS is unable to put the "brakes" on anxious arousal. If this happens, your brain and body remain on constant high alert.

OBSERVE

For the next three days, track your stress by noting some simple details. Record the following details during or after each stressful situation.

Date: ______________________ Time: __________

The stressful incident or thought: ______________________

Was your PNS or SNS activated? ______________________

Did you freeze or go into fight-or-flight mode? ______________

How long did it take you to return to equilibrium? __________

Date: ______________________ Time: __________

The stressful incident or thought: ______________________

Was your PNS or SNS activated? ______________________

Did you freeze or go into fight-or-flight mode? ______________

How long did it take you to return to equilibrium? __________

Date: ______________________ Time: __________

The stressful incident or thought: ______________________

Was your PNS or SNS activated? ______________________

Did you freeze or go into fight-or-flight mode? ______________

How long did it take you to return to equilibrium? __________

Date: ______________________ Time: __________

The stressful incident or thought: ______________________

Was your PNS or SNS activated? ______________________

Did you freeze or go into fight-or-flight mode? ______________________

How long did it take you to return to equilibrium? __________

Date: ______________________ Time: __________

The stressful incident or thought: ______________________

Was your PNS or SNS activated? ______________________

Did you freeze or go into fight-or-flight mode? ______________________

How long did it take you to return to equilibrium? __________

Date: ______________________ Time: __________

The stressful incident or thought: ______________________

Was your PNS or SNS activated? ______________________

Did you freeze or go into fight-or-flight mode? ______________________

How long did it take you to return to equilibrium? __________

REFLECT

What does the above exercise illuminate about how your nervous system responds to stress? Did having more of an awareness of your PNS and SNS help you move through the stress more quickly?

CHANGE

In what ways might having a greater awareness of your nervous system help you manage stressful situations? Help you return to equilibrium faster?

Your Body on Stress

Your stress response consists of a cascade of chemicals that travel rapidly through your body, sending messages to your organs and glands, your large muscles, and even your immune system. Over time, stress can affect your brain, your heart, your weight, your resistance to disease, and even your genetic makeup. Ongoing worry and anxiety can exacerbate your stress and diminish your body's ability to rest and recover.

How you view your stress matters. If you can find a way to lighten your load psychologically, your brain and body will be more resistant to stress, and your stressors won't get under your skin as much.

OBSERVE

How is your ongoing stress affecting you physically? Think about things like your energy levels, your weight or metabolism, your aches and pains, and your vulnerability to allergies, asthma, or other diseases. Also consider your habits and behavior—overusing substances, over- or undereating, sleeping too much or too little, or other ways you may numb yourself from stress. What effects are your physical symptoms or numbing actions having on your life?

REFLECT

What healthy strategies do you use now to combat the effects of your stress? List methods that you know have been shown to improve your sense of wellness and create calm: things like exercise, relaxation, regular meals, time spent with friends or loved ones, and so on.

- ____
- ____
- ____
- ____
- ____
- ____
- ____
- ____
- ____
- ____

As an additional step, you might reflect on strategies you've tried that don't work for you, such as quick fixes (like numbing out with substances or devices), so you can attempt to avoid those patterns.

- ______________________________
- ______________________________
- ______________________________
- ______________________________
- ______________________________
- ______________________________
- ______________________________
- ______________________________
- ______________________________
- ______________________________

CHANGE

How can you increase your use of healthy strategies, such as using them more often or in new situations? Are there any new strategies you might like to try to help you become more physically resilient under stress? How could you reduce your use of unhealthy strategies? What are your high-risk situations or mindsets for using unhealthy strategies? Make a specific plan or plans for these types of situations or states of mind.

Your Changeable Brain

Your brain contains billions of *neurons*—specialized cells that communicate with each other. Over time, any neurons and neural pathways you don't use weaken and wither away, while the ones you use most often become stronger—just like your muscles. Your brain also has the ability to grow new neurons from stem cells. This ability to change allows your brain's structure and wiring to be molded by experience, a quality known as *neuroplasticity*.

A famous saying (attributed to neuroscientist Donald Hebb) is "Neurons that fire together, wire together." That is, when a set of neurons gets activated, they become more closely linked, and the next time you're in the same situation, the same sequence of activation is more likely to repeat. In this way, your thoughts, feelings, and actions can actually change the structure of your brain over time. This explains why your childhood environment can affect your response to stress decades later. It also gives you the potential to change old behaviors that don't help you meet your present-day challenges. You can literally rewire your brain!

Repeatedly practicing new ways of thinking and behaving can actually change the neural pathways and chemicals in your brain.

OBSERVE

Reflect on some examples of neuroplasticity in your life. These could be everyday things you do all the time—learning a new word, remembering the name of somebody you met yesterday—and stuff that's more complex: learning a new skill, practicing meditation, doing challenging brain activities like crosswords, or starting and keeping to a new habit or lifestyle routine.

REFLECT

How difficult or easy were these things to learn or do? How long did it take? How much effort did it require?

CHANGE

Is neuroplasticity a new concept for you, or do you already incorporate activities and practices into your life with the intention of the forming new pathways and connections in the brain? If it's a new concept, how might you incorporate activities that support neuroplasticity into your day-to-day life? If you deliberately try to increase neuroplasticity, how might you strengthen or improve what you do?

Calming the Amygdala Emergency

Mindfulness of the Breath

Mindfulness is defined as a way of paying attention purposefully and with nonjudgmental acceptance to your present-moment experience. Mindfulness is both a practice and an approach to living that can help you better deal with stress. It helps create a calm, relaxed state of mind that prompts your parasympathetic nervous system to calm the fight-flight-or-freeze response. Repeated practice of mindfulness over weeks or months may even change the structure of your amygdala.

Here, you'll learn a mindful breathing practice to help you focus on your breath in a mindful way. First, though, take some time for reflection.

OBSERVE

Notice if your mind resists the idea of change by creating judgmental thoughts, such as *I won't be able to keep it up* or *It won't do any good*. You don't have to believe your judgmental thoughts; just notice them. Write down these resistant thoughts.

REFLECT

Review your mind's list of judgmental thoughts. See if you can replace your mind's judgmental attitude with one of curiosity. How could each resistant thought be framed in a way that is more open-minded and less judgmental? For example, you might reframe *I won't be able to keep it up* to *Can I stay focused on one full breath from the very beginning of the inhale to the very end of the exhale?*

Practice: Mindful Breathing

There's no right or wrong way to do this practice. Try to accept whatever your individual experience is. Also, there's no goal here. It's normal for your mind to wander. The practice is about noticing when this happens and bringing your mind back to the present moment.

Pick a comfortable, quiet place where you won't be disturbed, and set a timer—say, for five minutes.

Sit on a cushion on the floor or on a chair, with your back and shoulders straight. Close your eyes, or maintain a soft, unfocused gaze.

Begin to notice your breathing, staying open and curious. Notice your breath as it enters your body and leaves it. Don't try to force or change your breath in any way. Just notice it.

Continue observing your breath until the timer goes off. At the end of the practice, notice how your mind and body feel, then slowly come back to the room.

CHANGE

Note what has changed for you, good or bad, after engaging in mindful breathing. Did any new sensations or thoughts arise?

Mindfulness is both an attitude toward living and a resilient-brain skill that reduces your amygdala's reactivity.

Mindfulness of the Senses

When your amygdala sounds the alarm bell, you lose touch with the present moment as your emergency response kicks in. When you deliberately focus attention on your senses, you move from a "doing," "getting," or "avoiding" mindset to an observer mindset, noticing and describing what's around you. This change helps you be more present and connected.

OBSERVE

Over the next few days, pay attention when you're hijacked by stress, and stop and tune into your senses. This practice is wonderful to do in nature, but you can do it just about anywhere, at any time. Note the following details:

Date: ______________________ **Time:** ______________

Notice what you see: What are the colors, textures, shapes, the quality of the light?

____

____

Notice what you hear: Focus on a specific sound you hear. What is its tone, pitch, and rhythm?

____

____

Notice what you smell: Is it earthy, sweet, fresh, faint, intense?

____

____

Notice what you feel: What is the temperature, texture of clothing, air movement, the feeling of the ground or your chair?

____

____

Date: ______________________ **Time:** ______________________

Notice what you see: What are the colors, textures, shapes, the quality of the light?

____

____

Notice what you hear: Focus on a specific sound you hear. What is its tone, pitch, and rhythm?

____

____

Notice what you smell: Is it earthy, sweet, fresh, faint, intense?

____

____

Notice what you feel: What is the temperature, texture of clothing, air movement, the feeling of the ground or your chair?

____

____

Date: ______________________ **Time:** ______________________

Notice what you see: What are the colors, textures, shapes, the quality of the light?

____

____

Notice what you hear: Focus on a specific sound you hear. What is its tone, pitch, and rhythm?

____

____

Notice what you smell: Is it earthy, sweet, fresh, faint, intense?

____

____

Notice what you feel: What is the temperature, texture of clothing, air movement, the feeling of the ground or your chair?

____

____

Date: ______________________ **Time:** ______________

Notice what you see: What are the colors, textures, shapes, the quality of the light?

____

____

Notice what you hear: Focus on a specific sound you hear. What is its tone, pitch, and rhythm?

____

____

Notice what you smell: Is it earthy, sweet, fresh, faint, intense?

____

____

Notice what you feel: What is the temperature, texture of clothing, air movement, the feeling of the ground or your chair?

____

____

REFLECT

What did you notice about your inner experience and your feelings of stress after paying attention to your senses? How do you feel inside your body? What's it like inside your chest, back, belly? Do you feel more calm or open after paying attention to your senses? Explain.

CHANGE

You don't have to be controlled by your stress response; you can redirect your focus, thereby gaining more control over your behavior when stressed. How and when might you practice mindfulness of the senses? List some situations where you want to remember to practice mindfulness of the senses.

Mindfulness in Your Everyday Life

Stress takes your mind away from the present moment as your amygdala focuses your attention on what will happen if you don't address the problems or complete the tasks in front of you. Your mind may get tired and murky; you may find yourself getting distracted or zoning out instead of focusing on what's most important. You may operate on automatic pilot as your heart races and your breathing shortens in fight-flight-or-freeze mode. You may have even written down some of these responses in the earlier prompts.

The STOP practice can help you ground yourself when you are stressed. You can do it as soon as you notice stress beginning to creep in. If you try it out now, you'll know how to do it when the time comes. You can even make a habit out of doing this practice when you first wake up. Instead of jumping out of bed, make time for the STOP practice. It'll help you start your day off on a mindful note.

Practice: STOP

Stop. Stop whatever you're doing, and bring your mind back to the present moment.

Take a breath. Take a few deep breaths to slow down your fight-flight-or-freeze response.

Observe. Begin to notice what you're feeling, thinking, and doing. What's going on in your body? Describe any bodily sensations (such as tightness in your throat or shoulders) you become aware of. Is there an emotion word you can use to describe these feelings (such as "angry" or "scared")? Try to stay in the moment with these feelings, and imagine sending your breath into the areas that feel tight, constricted, or activated by these feelings.

Proceed. When you're feeling sufficiently present and aware, go about your business in a deliberate way. You may want to simply continue what you were doing.

OBSERVE

In what ways are you already integrating mindfulness into your life? And how might you integrate the STOP practice into your daily life? What body sensations, thoughts, or feelings will remind you to practice it?

REFLECT

What would it be like to be able to watch your stress from a state of calm? Describe in detail a clear way to deal with it as opposed to your usual reaction.

CHANGE

If you're not already practicing mindfulness, how might you incorporate it into your daily life? If you are, how can you increase your use of it? In what situations will practicing mindfulness be especially helpful for you?

Mindfulness has the potential to make you more stress-proof.

Grounding

Grounding strategies are things you can do to help you feel solid, soothed, and connected with your surroundings. They help you regain a sense of safety and normalcy when you feel overwhelmed by stress. You can deliberately move your body or focus on your body's position in space; focus on your sense of touch, taste, smell, sight, or sound; or do an activity that engages your logical mind or helps you express yourself. You might simply imagine yourself in an anchored state, connected to the earth. Grounding takes you out of fight-flight-or-freeze mode by signaling to your amygdala that you're safe in the present moment.

OBSERVE

How do you know when you're in a fight-flight-or-freeze response? What do you notice in your body and mind?

REFLECT

What actions are soothing and grounding to you that you can call on when stressed? These are often activities that involve deliberately directing your attention to some aspect of your experience that's not threatening. Some examples include:

- Doing the STOP practice
- Walking barefoot and feeling the connection between your feet and the carpet, grass, or sand on the beach
- Describing things in the room in terms of their sensory qualities (color, shape, texture, smell)
- Doing the four-count breath: Breathe in for a count of four, hold your breath for a count of four, breathe out for a count of four, and then pause for a count of four.
- Drinking a cup of tea slowly
- Smelling a calming essential oil, such as lavender
- Drawing, painting, or coloring
- Walking in or visualizing a peaceful place in nature
- Doing a small task that you find satisfying
- Taking a warm shower or bath
- Reading poetry
- Doing a jigsaw puzzle
- Listening to soothing music

Which grounding strategies do you currently use when you're stressed? Which grounding strategy or strategies work best for you? What new grounding strategies could you try? In what situations? How might they change your reactions?

CHANGE

What physical changes did you notice after trying a new grounding strategy? Maybe your breath lengthened or your heart rate slowed. What feeling or emotion changes did you notice after grounding?

Allowing In Your Emotions

Emotions grow, reach a peak, and then gradually subside. If you can acknowledge them without letting them sweep you away, they'll begin to pass. The trick is to notice them without identifying with them. When you allow in your emotions, you soften and slow them down so your prefrontal cortex has time to get on board. This makes it less likely that stress-related fear or anger will send you into a tailspin of impulsive action or flood your mind and body with panic.

Allowing in stressful emotions combines mindful awareness with a sense of exploration, curiosity, and self-compassion. Crucially, it's not pushing emotions away or changing them. It is letting them be there while you focus on noticing and describing them, rather than acting automatically.

To accept emotions means to be willing to experience them, even if they're uncomfortable or unwanted. It's being willing to accept the present moment and all that comes with it.

OBSERVE

Think about a stressful situation you're currently facing. How does that situation make you feel in your body? Notice any areas of discomfort, tightness, or tingling. Where are they located—in your head, neck, shoulders, chest, solar plexus, belly, feet, or other parts of your body? Notice any feelings of anxiety, panic, or being "speeded up." Describe these sensations in words.

REFLECT

Now attach an emotion word to the bodily sensations. Are you experiencing fear, anger, sadness, guilt, shame, or something else? (You may also be feeling a mixture of emotions.) Write down what you're feeling. Are you identifying with the emotion in any way? Do you have an aversion or resistance to the emotion? Do you tend to push away the emotion? Avoid it? Change it?

Now write: "It's okay to let myself feel this emotion."
If it feels helpful, you can even name the emotion: for example, "It's okay to let myself feel sadness."

CHANGE

Focus again on your body and notice whether the emotion you're experiencing has changed or stayed the same. Stay with the emotion for a few moments. Do you notice any softening? A sense of allowing in the emotion? A sense of expansion instead of constriction?

Emotion Surfing

You can't stop the waves of emotion from coming, but you can learn to surf those waves so you don't get knocked down by them. Surfing the waves of your emotions can help you remember that emotions don't go on forever and their effects will pass.

OBSERVE

Begin by thinking of a stressful situation. Bring to mind a clear image that represents the most important aspect of the stressor. What sensations do you feel in your body (tightness, constriction, unease)? Where do you feel these sensations?

Rate the intensity of your feeling
from neutral (0) to extremely intense (10).

0 - 1 - 2 - 3 - 4 - 5 - 6 - 7 - 8 - 9 - 10

REFLECT

Keep observing the feeling in your body while continuing to breathe. See if you can simply notice the feeling and adopt an open, accepting, curious attitude toward it. Like a surfer riding a wave, stay with the emotion with that welcoming attitude. Staying with it may take some practice. See if you can stay focused without overidentifying with the emotion or getting dragged into it. If you notice any tightness or tension, send some breath into that part of your body. Keep on noticing—keep surfing the feeling—for several minutes.

How would you rate the intensity now,
from neutral (0) to extremely intense (10)?

0 - 1 - 2 - 3 - 4 - 5 - 6 - 7 - 8 - 9 - 10

CHANGE

How did the intensity change as you took the time to notice and accept the feeling? Did the feeling get more intense, rise to a crescendo, and then gradually fade away, like a wave in the ocean?

How might the metaphor of surfing the wave of an emotion help you face, accept, or allow in emotions?

By looking at our own inner experiences with a curious, nonjudgmental, and welcoming attitude, we can learn to better tolerate negative states of mind—such as feeling stressed—and relate to these experiences in a kinder, more accepting way.

Softening and Soothing Emotions

Having a stress-proof brain means that you can experience emotions about your stressful situation in a balanced way, without letting the fight-flight-or-freeze mode take over and throw you off balance or cause you to act unwisely.

Knowing how to soften and soothe your stress-related emotions so you can hear their message more calmly and clearly can be advantageous. Mental imagery can help calm your amygdala's response and the fearful or angry emotions it creates.

OBSERVE

Again, think about a stressful situation you're currently facing. Picture an image that represents the most important aspect of the situation. Focus on the image until it's really clear. Notice how that image makes you feel in your body. This time, try to locate the exact sensation and describe it in words: for example, a lump in my throat, heat in my head.

REFLECT

Consider what emotion the sensation is signaling. Notice where you feel it in your body. What is it like? What color would it be if it had a color? And what shape? Is it large, medium, or small? Heavy or light? If it has edges, are they smooth or jagged? And how does the emotion feel—warm or cold? Rough or smooth? Is the emotion still or is it moving? If it's moving, does it move quickly or slowly?

CHANGE

Now visualize the emotion in your body in terms of these qualities. You might imagine a heavy gray blob, a green puddle of goo, a broken heart, or streaks of light. Use mental imagery and your intuitive sense to give form and sensory qualities to the emotion.

Next, try to find a way to soften the emotion. If the edges are jagged, can you smooth them out? If the emotion is heavy, can you make it lighter? If it's large, can you shrink it a bit? You might also imagine softening the shape at the edges or wrapping it up in a soft cloud-like material. You might ask it what it needs and see whether you can get an answer.

What methods did you try? If you were able to soften the emotion, does it feel less dense, less intense, or less threatening than when you began?

Expressing Your Thoughts and Emotions

Creating a written narrative that integrates the facts of a stressful situation with thoughts and emotions often has a grounding effect, which helps your amygdala calm down so you can act more effectively. Writing in twenty- to thirty-minute increments is a way to focus on and externalize your emotions about the stressor.

(Be sure to take care of yourself. If you have experienced a serious trauma such as sexual abuse, and have very intense feelings about it or are highly avoidant of it, you may want to consult with a mental health professional before trying this exercise.)

OBSERVE

Write about an ongoing or unresolved stressful situation you're facing. Present the situation as a narrative story with a beginning, middle, and end, maybe adding dialogue, setting details, character traits, or other story elements. Don't worry about spelling, handwriting, or grammar. The most important thing is to link the facts of the event with your corresponding deepest thoughts and emotions.

REFLECT

Did this practice of writing about the situation in story format offer any clarity, insights, or new perspective? Did you find this practice grounding in any way? Did it encourage you to be proactive in creating and pursuing goals related to the stressful situation?

CHANGE

How might the practice of expressive writing be different from journaling? How might you integrate the practice of expressive writing—telling a story—into your life in the future?

Reframing Your View of Stress

How you view your stressor is just as important as your actual circumstances. Acute stress can energize you to perform your best and even help you grow new neurons. It keeps the brain alert and improves physical and mental performance. The secret is to find a way to see your stressful situation as at least partially under your control and to feel more confident in your skills and coping abilities.

OBSERVE

Recall a time when you got excited about something. Describe how you felt physically and mentally.

What are the similarities between how you feel when excited and how you feel when stressed?

REFLECT

Describe your feelings of aversion and your negative judgments about stress. What stresses you out about stress?

CHANGE

Could you view your stress as a normal part of life? As a challenge rather than a threat? Even as beneficial or useful? For each aversion or judgment you just wrote about, reframe the statement to view stress in a neutral or even positive way. Take into consideration any similarities you noticed between excitement and stress.

Stress that you can control or master has an "inoculation" effect. Overcoming some level of stress and adversity can make us more resilient in the future.

Finding Confidence

When you feel confident that you can manage your stress, you'll feel less stressed. Consciously bring to mind experiences or times when you mastered stress leading to increased confidence and a sense of control.

OBSERVE

Consider a stressful situation you're facing. On a scale of 0 (no confidence) to 10 (complete confidence), rate your level of confidence in your ability to manage the situation.

0 - 1 - 2 - 3 - 4 - 5 - 6 - 7 - 8 - 9 - 10

Explain your rating. Why do you believe that you can or can't manage this situation effectively?

REFLECT

Reflect on major or chronic stress, trauma, or adversity that you've experienced in the past. What skills, efforts, people, resources, or personal qualities helped you get through it? How can you apply those to help in your current situation?

CHANGE

Again, rate your current level of confidence in your ability to manage the situation on a scale of 0 (no confidence) to 10 (complete confidence).

0 - 1 - 2 - 3 - 4 - 5 - 6 - 7 - 8 - 9 - 10

Is there any change since your first rating? Explain.

Having a role model who faced the same difficulties and coped successfully can boost your confidence. Reach out and ask for advice.

Focusing on the Things You Can Control

The need to feel in control is hardwired into the human brain. To the amygdala, lack of control and unpredictability are threats to survival—which results in the stress response. This is another example of the reality that how you perceive your stress is just as important as the actual circumstances. When you can find some way to perceive control over your stressful circumstances—even just a small part—you'll be less likely to be negatively affected by the situation and more likely to cope effectively. If you find yourself ruminating about the uncontrollable aspects of a situation, either deliberately focus on the controllable stuff or get up and do something else.

OBSERVE

Consider different aspects of the stressful situation that you're facing. Make a list of the following:

Things you can control:

- ________________
- ________________
- ________________
- ________________
- ________________
- ________________
- ________________
- ________________
- ________________
- ________________

Things you can't control:

-
-
-
-
-
-
-
-
-
-

Things you're not sure you can control:

-
-
-
-
-
-
-
-
-
-

REFLECT

How can you address the controllable aspects? What uncontrollable aspects can you learn to accept?

CHANGE

When can you schedule specific times to work on changing the controllable aspects?

What obstacles might you face? Make a plan for overcoming them.

You can't always control what you feel or think, but you can control what you do!

Containing the Things You Can't Control

Another strategy that can be helpful with the stuff you can't control is to deliberately move your attention away from these aspects so you can focus on doing the best job you can with the stuff that *is* controllable. Of course, you can't completely control your worries, but you can let your amygdala know you have the uncontrollable stuff contained. That way, your brain will be less likely to remind you of everything that might go wrong!

Practice: Containing Things You Can't Control

If you could hold your worries and fears about the uncontrollable parts of your stressor in a container of some sort, what sort would you choose? A big oak barrel or a sturdy trunk? A metal safe? A large vase?

- Once you have decided on a container, bring up a mental picture of it. Be very specific about its size, shape, color, and texture. You may want to imagine labeling your container with a description, such as "Fears About My Divorce." You can also imagine writing or drawing on the container or decorating it in whatever way you choose.
- Imagine putting all your worries and fears about uncontrollable outcomes of your stress into the container. Visualize yourself packing them in, or see your worries as a stream of smoke, light, sand, or water that flows into the container. Give them the form that feels right to you.
- Once all your worries are in the container, imagine sealing it. You could use a lid, a lock, chains, plastic wrap, or all of these. It's up to you. When your container is sealed tight, imagine storing it somewhere. You could bury it deep underground, put it in a cave, stow it in an attic, load it onto a boat, or send it into space in a rocket ship. Anywhere you want to store it is okay.
- When your container is sealed and stored, imagine yourself walking away from it and back into your life. You can come back and open it if you need to, but for now it's safely put away.
- Set an intention to focus your effort and energy on the parts of your stressor that you can control.

OBSERVE

Once you've completed the practice, jot down a few notes about the experience. What was it like? What type of container did you use? What did you put in it? Where did you put the container after sealing it? Did you have any resistance to putting your worries in?

REFLECT

How do you feel after completing this practice? What did it teach you? Did you notice any sense of containment of the uncontrollable stuff? Did it help you limit its intrusion into your life?

CHANGE

What will you carry forward from this exercise? Do you feel a new sense of freedom to devote your time and energy to things you can control?

Think about what is most important and meaningful in your life. When your life feels full and meaningful despite your stress, you'll feel a greater sense of control over your life circumstances.

Building Stress Resilience

Research shows that overcoming some stress and adversity can make us more resilient in the future. If you can experience a sense of control and feel good about your achievements in one area of your life, then stress in other areas won't drag you down as much. Try to find a hobby, activity, or sport that gives you a sense of accomplishment. Perceiving control over at least some part of your circumstances can help make you less physically and psychologically reactive to stress.

OBSERVE

Identify an aspect of your life unrelated to the stressor in which you can grow. Think about a sport, a hobby, an activity, or a relationship that's important to you—ideally something you can focus on for twenty minutes to an hour or two at a time. It could be volunteer work, art, writing, baking or cooking, running, hiking, joining a yoga class, meditating, spending time with your partner (or parent or child), or anything else that's personally important to you. What are some of these areas? How might they help you grow, and what do you value about them?

REFLECT

Now choose one activity that you can devote some time to regularly over the next month, one that would create a sense of self-worth and positive achievement for you. Record the details of the activity and how you will schedule it into your month. Also include the signs that will indicate you are making progress.

CHANGE

After you've done the activity for a month, come back to this journal and reflect on how it went. Were you able to achieve what you set out to do? Can you allow yourself to be proud of that? Did you notice any change in your overall level of stress? Would it be worthwhile to continue prioritizing progress—in your chosen activity or other areas of your life—in order to increase your resilience to stress?

Overcoming Perfectionism

Do you find that you often pressure yourself to work harder, go faster, and not take breaks? Do you often think, *I'm not doing enough!* and then berate yourself for not having enough self-discipline and willpower? If so, you may have perfectionistic tendencies. Perfectionism can result from a rigid mindset in which you don't adjust your expectations to fit situations.

Although it's important to try to meet deadlines and solve problems, this sense of pressure can lead you to be too hard on yourself. Never letting up or giving yourself a break can turn acute stress (such as when you're facing a work deadline) into chronic stress. Perfectionism adds layers of unnecessary stress to already stressful situations. Rather than calming your amygdala down, perfectionism riles it up.

OBSERVE

Using this scale, rate how much you agree or disagree with each statement: 1 = completely disagree, 2 = mostly disagree, 3 = somewhat disagree, 4 = neither agree nor disagree, 5 = somewhat agree, 6 = mostly agree, and 7 = completely agree.

_______ No matter how hard I work, I always feel as if I could be doing more.

_______ There are no excuses for making mistakes.

_______ I give my very best in everything I do.

_______ If things aren't done perfectly, it feels as if they're not done at all.

_______ I always check and recheck my work.

_______ If my house isn't organized and tidy, I can't relax.

_______ Being tired is no excuse for taking a break when there's work to be done.

If you mostly agreed or completely agreed with more than two statements, perfectionism may be a problem for you.

REFLECT

Reflecting on your responses to the questions above, where does perfectionism show up for you? Do you overestimate the negative consequences of making a mistake? Do you proofread or check your work more than necessary? Describe how perfectionism influences a particular task or project.

CHANGE

How might you set limits with yourself to let some perfectionism go? Consider the task or project you reflected on. Could you give yourself a set amount of time to work on it, or, if there are decisions to be made, give yourself a time limit for those? Set an alarm for your maximum allowed time, and when the alarm goes off, force yourself to get up and move on, even if you're not finished. (If you feel the need, you can schedule time at the end of the day for high-priority tasks that you didn't finish.)

Afterward, come back to this journal. Did you notice any increase in efficiency in your work when you gave yourself a time limit? Is this a strategy you want to continue with this particular task or other tasks and projects?

Overcoming Guilt

Just as perfectionism is unhelpful under conditions of stress, so is guilt. Guilt is an emotion we often learn in childhood, when our caregivers say things like, "Eat all your food; lots of children in this country don't have enough food," and "I've been working my fingers to the bone to take care of you, and all you do is complain." We internalize these messages, and as adults, we feel as if we can never do enough.

Stress can also trigger feelings of guilt when there's not enough time to get everything done. We may have to choose between meeting our own goals or doing things for others. Other kinds of stressors, such as ending a relationship or having to step away from someone who's toxic to us, can make us feel guilty because someone else may be upset with our decision.

Finally, our culture sends us strong messages about not being selfish and self-indulgent. Unfortunately, people get confused and interpret these messages in an all-or-nothing way. If you lied to someone you care about or acted in a selfish and hurtful way, feeling guilt can motivate you to stop the hurtful behavior. This change will likely improve your relationships and your self-esteem. Other types of guilt are likely to be counterproductive and make you feel more stressed. When you're stressed, you certainly don't need the additional burden of unnecessary guilt!

Take a step back, give yourself a break, allow yourself just to do what's most important, and allow time for rest, rather than trying to do everything all the time.

OBSERVE

Using this scale, rate how much you agree or disagree with each statement: 1 = completely disagree, 2 = mostly disagree, 3 = somewhat disagree, 4 = neither agree nor disagree, 5 = somewhat agree, 6 = mostly agree, and 7 = completely agree.

_______ I don't feel good when I put myself first.

_______ If I'm not working or being productive all the time, I feel lazy.

_______ I never feel as if I'm doing enough for the people in my life.

_______ I need to look after others before I can take care of my own needs.

_______ If I eat out, I feel guilty because I could be saving the money.

_______ Even though I spend most of my time with my kids or working, I feel I need to do more.

_______ I feel guilty complaining about my stress because others have it worse.

If you mostly agreed or completely agreed with more than two statements, unnecessary guilt may be a problem for you.

REFLECT

If you feel guilty because you're not doing enough for your kids, partner, or family, make a list of all the things you regularly do for them. Then make another list that includes all the things you do to take care of yourself when you're stressed.

Which list is longer? If your "do for others" list is as long as or longer than your "do for myself" list, could you reframe your perspective and realize that you are doing enough for others and don't have reason to feel guilty? If your "do for myself" list is longer, how do the self-care activities help you be a better parent, partner, or family member?

CHANGE

For the next week, write a "self-gratitude" diary at the end of every day, noting at least three things you did that day that furthered your goals, improved your health and happiness, reflected your personal values, or helped someone you care about.

At the end of the week, read what you've written. Then come back to this journal and consider how it felt to focus on your accomplishments or good deeds. How might this sort of gratitude practice help you manage feelings of guilt?

Learning new ways of doing things is often challenging and takes time, so be patient with yourself and with the process. It takes months, not days, to really change your brain.

Practicing Self-Compassion

Self-compassion—the ability to be kind to yourself, to realize you're only human and don't have to be perfect—can help you adapt to major life events, disappointments, and chronic stressors. Self-compassion is like a soothing balm to your amygdala. It sends the message to your brain that you're not under imminent threat and don't have to use an emergency response. Rather, you can take your time, relax, and give your prefrontal cortex a chance to respond. As a result, your amygdala sends a signal to terminate the stress response.

One way to enhance your self-compassion is through meditation. Loving-kindness meditation, or *metta*, is a Buddhist teaching to develop qualities of altruistic love.

Practice: Loving-Kindness Meditation

Sit quietly with your legs crossed and maintain an upright and relaxed pose. Begin to notice your breathing and let your mind and body settle. Take a few slow breaths, noticing your inhalations and exhalations.

Think about the stress you're facing. Try to get a visual image of your stressed self. What do you feel in your body? What does your posture look like? What thoughts fill your mind? What's the expression on your face? Imagine yourself rushing around or worrying. As you contemplate this image, become aware of the suffering that the stress is causing you and of your deep wish to be at ease and at peace.

Now think about somebody past or present, real or imaginary, who loves and cares about you deeply. Imagine this person looking at you with deep caring and compassion. And imagine them saying to you:

> **Dear** *(insert your name here)***,**
>
> ***I see how stressed and tired you are. How much you suffer with your feelings of stress. How anxious and overwhelmed you feel. And I send these wishes to you:***
>
> ***May you be healthy.***
>
> ***May you be safe and secure.***
>
> ***May you be at peace with yourself and others.***
>
> ***May you live with ease and happiness.***

After saying this a few times, bid farewell to your loved one.

Now imagine saying these same words to yourself. Say them a few times and notice how it feels to hear these kind wishes expressed toward you. If you feel any discomfort or self-consciousness, let those feelings be there. Notice any resistance you have to wishing yourself well. As you keep practicing metta, the resistance will lessen. It's not important that you believe the words right now. It's just important that you say them.

Once you're comfortable expressing metta to yourself, you can extend it to include

> family members who are also affected by your stress;
>
> friends and colleagues who face the stress with you;
>
> difficult people in your life who cause stress for you;
>
> all living beings who deal with stress and suffering.

Notice these people in their state of stress and then send them loving-kindness. Remember to bring up a visual image of each person or group before you say the phrases. You may have difficulty wishing metta to people who seem to be the source of your stress. But if they didn't suffer as much and were more at ease, they would cause less stress for you! If you can't yet wish them well out of compassion or tolerance for them, it's okay to send metta to them for these "selfish" reasons.

OBSERVE

How did it feel to hear these kind wishes expressed toward you? What was it like for you to wish yourself well? What was it like to wish metta to people you care about and those who seem to be the source of your stress?

REFLECT

Rather than compounding your stress by worrying, blaming, or criticizing yourself, you can calm down your amygdala by treating yourself with kindness and understanding. When you face highly stressful situations or losses, your natural tendency might be to ask yourself what you did wrong. Instead, saying to yourself *I did the best I could given what I knew at the time* can help you feel better and give you more courage to face your stressors and persist when things get tough. What reminders could you use to treat yourself with self-compassion?

CHANGE

Consider this quote associated with the Buddha's teachings: "You yourself, as much as anybody in the entire universe, deserve your love and affection." How does this idea land with you? In what ways can you strengthen your self-compassion, perhaps in terms of a daily meditation practice or intention? Write down some affirmations of self-love to inspire you.

Asking Your Inner Critic to Step Aside

Constantly berating yourself for not doing enough will just make you more stressed. Although you may get more stuff done, you'll tax your health and your self-esteem. What if you asked your inner critic to step aside and make room for a more compassionate presence so you can become a loving advocate for yourself?

OBSERVE

Tune in and listen to your inner critic for a moment. What judgmental and critical things do you hear? Perhaps that you're a loser or not competent, that you've made a mess of your life, or that you're going to fail. How does it feel to hear these unkind words when you're feeling stressed and trying to do your best?

REFLECT

Now put a face to this critical voice. Perhaps it's the face of one of your parents, teachers, coaches, or romantic partners who used to speak to you in this way. Or it might be the face of an imaginary being, such as a witch or an animal, a wolf or an alligator. Whatever it looks like is okay. Picture the critic standing there berating you.

Now bring into the image a wise person or being who cares deeply about you. It can be someone from your past or present, a spiritual figure (such as Jesus or the Buddha), or an imaginary creature. It may be someone you knew well or someone you didn't know well but knew to be a good person. It can even be a character from a book, movie, or TV show. Imagine that this being, seeing you listening to your inner critic, is filled with love and compassion for you.

Imagine the compassionate being stepping between you and the critic and holding up a hand, telling the critic kindly but firmly to stop. How does the compassionate being tell the critic that the way it's behaving is hurting you or causing you stress? How does this compassionate being explain that the critic needs to speak to you with kindness?

Then, imagine the compassionate being comforting you with physical gestures and kind, encouraging words. What does this compassionate being do and say to you? What do you feel in your mind and body as you feel the compassion and words of encouragement?

CHANGE

Now imagine the compassionate being becoming a part of you so that you'll always have this inner being to protect and support you. What does it feel like to have someone stand up for you and encourage you? What would your life be like if you had such an advocate with you all the time?

Engaging the Cortex to Stop the Stress Cycle

Developing Cognitive Flexibility

Cognitive flexibility is a mental capacity that helps you look at a situation from multiple perspectives, make sense of conflicting information, and adjust your responses based on changes in the situation as it unfolds. It helps you take a new tack when the old one isn't working. Cognitive flexibility is an essential skill in successfully negotiating stress.

Think of cognitive flexibility as working with mental clay; you can mold your brain in different ways until you find a way of thinking and coping that best fits the situation. Cognitive rigidity, by comparison, is like working with cement, and cognitive chaos is like working with sand falling through your fingers.

OBSERVE

Think about a stressful situation you're currently facing, and answer these questions:

Do you see it as a threat, a challenge, a loss, or all of the these?

____

____

What do you have to lose?

____

____

What do you have to learn?

What are your priorities and goals in dealing with this situation?

How controllable do you think the situation is?

How might it change over time?

What are some possible outcomes?

Do you need to modify your view of the situation, priorities, or goals to deal with these potential changes?

REFLECT

Think about the other person (or people) involved in the situation (including the person you're having conflict with, if appropriate), and answer these questions:

What's their view of the situation?

Do they see it as a threat, a challenge, or a loss?

What are their most pressing priorities and goals?

Is there anything you can do to reach a compromise or work together with them, or do you need to set better boundaries for yourself?

CHANGE

Try to find the most objective viewpoint, and answer these questions:

How might a neutral observer see the situation?

How might they see your role in the stressor? What do they see you doing that is helping or hurting?

How might they see the other people's roles and contribution?

What, if anything, can you learn from considering these different viewpoints? Are there any new perspectives or strategies that might be helpful to you? What internal or external barriers do you need to overcome? How might you implement them?

Moving On from Worry and Rumination

Worry and *rumination* are two common but unproductive responses to stress. Worry can magnify the stressor by bringing up more and more negative possibilities. One negative thought leads to another, and you start feeling more and more stressed. Worry makes you feel as if the worst is already happening. Rumination is persistent and repetitive worry, in which you revisit the same information repeatedly without finding any new answers.

It's very difficult to distinguish helpful ways of thinking about your stressors from unhelpful ones. Your brain will try to convince you that you're helping yourself by worrying and ruminating. In reality, worry and rumination are the result of a feedback loop between your amygdala and your prefrontal cortex. When your amygdala sends out its alarm signals, your prefrontal cortex analyzes the alarm (worry), and then, instead of calming down your amygdala, comes up with other things that might go wrong. This creates a vicious cycle of escalating and self-perpetuating alarm and worry between your amygdala and your prefrontal cortex.

OBSERVE

For one week, notice and record the triggers that make you worry or ruminate (such as talking to another anxious person, lying awake in bed, or watching TV). Answer these questions about each worry:

Date: ______________________ Time: ______________

What is the trigger that makes you worry? What is the worry?

How helpful is the worry?

Are you actually finding new solutions and making concrete plans to implement them?

Are you seeing the situation in a new light or in a more positive way?

Do you feel better after thinking about the problem in this way, or do you feel worse?

Date: ______________________________ Time: ________________

What is the trigger that makes you worry? What is the worry?

____

____

____

How helpful is the worry?

____

____

Are you actually finding new solutions and making concrete plans to implement them?

____

____

Are you seeing the situation in a new light or in a more positive way?

____

Do you feel better after thinking about the problem in this way, or do you feel worse?

____

____

Date: ______________________ Time: ____________

What is the trigger that makes you worry? What is the worry?

How helpful is the worry?

Are you actually finding new solutions and making concrete plans to implement them?

Are you seeing the situation in a new light or in a more positive way?

Do you feel better after thinking about the problem in this way, or do you feel worse?

Date: ______________________ Time: ____________

What is the trigger that makes you worry? What is the worry?

How helpful is the worry?

Are you actually finding new solutions and making concrete plans to implement them?

Are you seeing the situation in a new light or in a more positive way?

Do you feel better after thinking about the problem in this way, or do you feel worse?

REFLECT

Come back to this journal after recording your worries over the week. For the most part, did worrying make you feel better or worse about your problem? Explain.

Short-term worry can be productive if it helps you plan and solve problems. Worry can also be helpful if it leads to new perspectives on the problem. But often worry turns into rumination.

CHANGE

If you aren't finding solutions and new perspectives and you feel worse, then the worry is unhelpful and you need to focus on something else. Choose one of these strategies to try the next time you catch yourself worrying or ruminating:

- If you're lying awake worrying at night, get up after fifteen minutes and read a book, listen to music, or watch TV.
- Schedule fun or distracting activities (going to the gym, walking in nature, doing jigsaws or word puzzles, doing organizational tasks, cooking, going out with friends, talking to a friend on the phone, and so on) during times when you would normally be ruminating.
- Picture your worries as bubbles popping in the air, clouds floating by, or leaves floating down a stream. This mindfulness technique can give you some distance from your worries.
- Create a "worry corner" in your house, or designate a chair as your "worry chair." Allow yourself to worry about your stressor only when you're in your worry chair or corner. Give yourself fifteen minutes two or three times a day to sit and worry. If worries come up at other times, either write them down or save them for your next worry period. Soon your brain will learn to associate worry only with your worry spot and associate all your other activities with the absence of worry. In this way, you can satisfy your urge to worry in a controlled, time-limited way.

- Find a funny image to focus on every time you start worrying, such as a bright pink elephant on roller skates. When you start to worry or ruminate, think of your elephant!
- Interrupt worry cycles by getting up and walking around or by mindfully checking in with what's happening in your body. If you notice an area of tension, send some breaths into that area to open up space or create a bit of softening. Try to give the tension a label, such as "fear," "anger," or "sadness." This can overcome the avoidance associated with being "in your head" and feeling disconnected from your surroundings or bodily sensations.

After you've tried out your chosen strategy a few times, return to this journal and record your experience. What was it like to try a worry- and rumination-stopping activity? How do you envision using such activities in your day-to-day life? How do you imagine these strategies will affect your days?

De-Catastrophizing

Catastrophizing is the thought process of magnifying how bad a stressor is and turning it into a catastrophe that's going to ruin your life. Catastrophizing also overestimates the likelihood of disastrous events. *De-catastrophizing* is knowing how to calm your amygdala using cognitive strategies from your prefrontal cortex and the left side of your brain, which is the seat of logic.

OBSERVE

Consider your stressor and answer these questions:

What am I afraid will happen? (Be very specific: for example, "I'll lose my job" or "My wife will leave me.")

How likely is it that this will happen?

Am I confusing thoughts (which are really guesses about what might happen) with facts?

What evidence do I have that these things will happen? Is there any evidence suggesting that they won't happen?

What's the best thing that could happen?

What's the worst thing that could happen?

What's most likely to happen? Why is this outcome most likely?

If the worst did happen, how bad would it be? On a scale of 0 to 100, with 100 being a loved one dying, what would I rate this event? ______

REFLECT

Consider what you wrote and answer these questions:

Could I survive the worst possible outcome?

If my family members are likely to be affected, could they survive it?

What aspects of our lives would stay the same, even if it happens? (For example, "We'd have to sell our house, but we'd still be able to buy or rent a house nearby.")

If the worst did happen, what strategies could I use to cope with it? What resources or sources of support could I rely on to help me get through it (friends or family, loans, government programs, and so on)?

CHANGE

Does the stressful event feel less like a catastrophe now? Explain.

Diagnosing Thinking Traps

In addition to overestimating how bad an event is and underestimating your ability to cope, there are other thinking traps that you can get caught up in when under stress. Stress makes us less cognitively flexible and more likely to see things in all-or-nothing ways.

These common thinking traps may be making you feel worse about your situation. You can mark the aspects of each trap that really speak to you.

- ***Black-and-white thinking***. Are you seeing things in black and white and forgetting about the gray? This kind of thinking tells you that either things are perfect or they're terrible; you're either a success or a failure—there's nothing in between.

- ***Emotional reasoning***. Do you assume something is true just because it feels true? For example, you think you're a loser or unlovable because it just feels that way. When you feel down or have been rejected, you're more likely to see yourself and others negatively without any evidence to support your views.

- ***Tunnel vision***. Do your feelings about the stressor dominate your life to the point where they're all you can focus on? Do you forget about the aspects of your life that the stressor doesn't affect? Do you become preoccupied with planning for something bad or trying to prevent it from happening?

- ***Wishful thinking***. Are you organizing your life around what you hope will happen, rather than preparing for different possible outcomes? Do you have a backup plan? Are you avoiding the reality of what's actually happening? With this kind of thinking, you may feel less stressed in the short run, but your failure to plan can make the stress worse later on. Beneath the wishful thinking, you're probably feeling a great deal of anxiety.
- ***Personalizing***. Are you interpreting the stressor too personally and seeing yourself as responsible for it, without any evidence? Often stressors happen because of factors beyond your control. Personalizing leads you to believe you did something wrong to cause a negative outcome, but that may not be the case.
- ***Blaming yourself or others***. Rather than focusing on the current situation and what you can do about it, do you blame yourself for past decisions that didn't work out? Or do you blame other people without taking responsibility for your contribution to the problem?
- ***Guilt and regret***. If you've acted against your values or hurt yourself and people you love, guilt can help you make amends. But once you've made amends, you need to forgive yourself. Otherwise, guilt will keep you from being mentally present for the people you love. If you're regretting a past decision, are you taking the prior circumstances into account? Did you have the same information that you have now?

- ***Pessimism***. When you think about your stressor, are you seeing the glass as half empty? When you feel stressed, your negative mood may prevent you from seeing the positive or neutral aspects of the situation. Pessimistic thinking makes you feel like giving up because all is lost, but mostly this isn't the case. When you focus on only the negative aspects of a stressful situation, you may start to feel depressed or not see the whole picture accurately.

- ***Overthinking and second-guessing yourself***. Every time you try to make a decision or take a course of action, do you begin to doubt yourself? Do you start thinking of all the negatives or things that could go wrong? Overthinking and second-guessing yourself can make you feel stuck.

- ***Unhelpful comparisons***. Do you compare yourself to others who seem to be doing better or coping better with stress? Perhaps other people have more money, more energy, more friends, or a better job or house. Comparing yourself to such people will make you feel worse about yourself and your situation. Know that other people's lives may not be what they seem, and your challenges may have created inner strengths you don't fully appreciate.

- ***Judging mind***. Do you judge and criticize yourself for not doing what you think you "should" be doing? Or tell yourself you should be doing more, but you don't actually do it? What are the real reasons that you're not taking the "perfect" steps to solve the problem?

OBSERVE

Think about a stressful situation you're facing and write a brief description of the facts of the situation. Remember, facts are things that actually happened or that somebody could observe. They don't include judgments, opinions, or predictions.

REFLECT

Write down your personal view of the situation: Why do you think it happened? What implications does it have for your life? What does it say about you and your abilities? What do you want to do about it? What's stopping you from acting? How do you think the situation is going to end? Write down any negative thoughts you have about yourself or others relating to this situation.

CHANGE

Read through what you've written and highlight or underline any parts of it that can be classified as one of the thinking traps above. List the sentences and the thinking traps you noticed.

Overcoming Thinking Traps

To alleviate your stress and prevent further damage to your self-esteem, you need to recognize your thinking traps when they're occurring, rather than continuing to believe what they tell you. Being able to recognize your thinking traps is a form of *metacognition*, or thinking about thinking.

OBSERVE

Considering what you learned about your own thinking traps in the prior exercise, how do thinking traps affect your view of stress and its impact on you?

REFLECT

Select one of the thinking traps you identified in the previous exercise—perhaps the one that showed up the most often—and reflect on the questions associated with that particular trap:

Black-and-white thinking:

- Am I thinking in absolutes?
- How do I find the gray?
- Can I see things from a more balanced perspective?
- How can I be less negative or judgmental?
- Can anything good can come out of a situation that I'm labeling "all bad"?
- How might I learn to adjust to the "bad" outcome if it happens?

Emotional reasoning:

- Is this true or does it just *feel* true?
- What are the facts of the situation—things I can observe, rather than thoughts, predictions, opinions, or emotions?
- Do I need to see this situation more objectively?

Tunnel vision:

- Am I overemphasizing one piece of the problem and ignoring the big picture?
- If I'm just focused on the negative, what positive aspects of my life am I ignoring?
- If I'm just seeing my weaknesses, what are my strengths?

Wishful thinking:

- Am I focusing on what I wish would happen rather than what's actually happening?
- Based on my past experience and current knowledge, what would I say is most likely to happen, and how can I best plan for it?
- What's my backup plan?

Personalizing:

- Am I taking things too personally or taking all the responsibility when other people or outside factors contributed to the situation?
- What would an objective observer say?
- Am I remembering that stress is a universal experience and a natural part of life, rather than a sign that I've messed up?

Blaming yourself or others:

- Am I blaming just one person when many different factors contributed?
- Am I being too hard on myself or others?
- Am I looking at the whole picture and taking the situational factors into account?
- How can I focus on dealing with the problem now rather than blaming?

Guilt and regret:

- What external factors influenced my decision?
- Did I feel frozen, panicked, or overwhelmed?
- What past experiences led me to act in this way?

- What do I know now that I didn't know then?
- Did I intentionally hurt anybody or fail to act when I should have?
- Did I do what I thought was best, given my capacities and knowledge at the time?
- How might I begin to let go and forgive myself?
- How can I stay focused on dealing with the present rather than looking back?

Pessimism:

- Am I seeing the glass as half empty?
- If a negative outcome happens, do I have coping strategies and sources of support to help me get through it?
- Can I frame the stressful situation in a more positive way?
- Are there any positive outcomes that could happen instead of the negative one I'm expecting?
- Is there a way to see myself and my actions or abilities in a more positive light?
- Is there anything meaningful or helpful I can take from the situation?

Overthinking and second-guessing yourself:

- Am I focusing on what could go wrong rather than what could go right?
- Am I looking for the perfect solution rather than the best choice given the current circumstances?
- Am I willing to accept some reasonable degree of risk and discomfort in order to move forward?

Unhelpful comparisons:

- Am I comparing how I feel to how other people seem to be doing?
- Are other people really doing that much better than I am?
- Did they start out with advantages or opportunities that I didn't have?
- Do I really know what their lives are like?
- Am I giving myself enough credit for what I've accomplished or the hard work I've put in?

Judging mind:

- Are my judging thoughts helpful or harmful? If they're harmful, can I direct my attention away from them?
- Is there a more compassionate and understanding way to view the situation?

If you're inspired, answer the questions associated with each thinking trap you listed in the prior exercise.

Did the process of exploring your thinking traps help you recognize that your thoughts are just thoughts and not facts? How will knowing that such thoughts are opinions and that you don't have to listen to them affect your view of stress?

CHANGE

The next time you notice yourself caught in a thinking trap, describe the process you'll use to identify and get out of the trap, to remember that your judging thoughts are just thoughts, or to focus on something positive.

Letting Go of Hypervigilance

Hypervigilance is an elevated state of being on high alert and extremely sensitive to your surroundings; it's also an evolutionary response to stress. It can include the anticipation of danger or threats and be accompanied by anxiety and overreactions. Your brain and body weren't designed to remain hyped up or numbed out in fight-flight-or-freeze mode over long periods of time. When they do, they don't get a chance to rest or recover, leading you to feel worn out.

OBSERVE

In what ways is your stress making you hypervigilant? Are you waiting for the other shoe to drop, feeling as if you can't let up even for a minute? What fears or doubts are driving your hypervigilance?

REFLECT

What effect does your hypervigilance have on your body, mind, and emotions?

In what ways is this elevated state affecting different areas of your life?

What would it mean to you to rest your brain? To give yourself a break from hypervigilance?

CHANGE

These three skills can redirect your focus away from hypervigilance and give your brain a rest:

1. **Let it be.** How might it be for you to let a situation be, without having to do something about it or monitor it all the time? When your amygdala sends your body into fight-flight-or-freeze mode, you experience an urge to act right away, even if that's not the best thing to do. Take a few deep breaths and slow things down. If trying to control the situation isn't productive, take a step back and just let it unfold. Or find a trusted friend or loved one to talk to so that you satisfy your urge to act (in this case, speak) without doing any damage by acting impulsively.

2. **Find distractions.** Instead of monitoring the stressor all the time, find something else to focus on. It might be a fun activity, a challenging task such as a word game, or a hobby such as crafting. You might focus on an uplifting news story, follow a TV series, read a book, or watch sports. You might organize your closets. You might interact with your pet, focus on your kids, or think about something funny or sexy.

3. **Resist your impulses.** This skill involves deliberately doing something other than what your amygdala's response tells you to do and using your prefrontal cortex to come up with a different intention and action. If your brain is telling you to constantly monitor your boyfriend's Facebook page, write in your diary instead. If you're tempted to drunk-text your girlfriend when you haven't heard back from her, go home and sleep it off instead. In this way, you're leading with your prefrontal cortex rather than your amygdala, and you're fighting the urge to act destructively in response to stress. This can help you protect your relationships and your health.

Over the next few days, practice one of these skills when you notice hypervigilance seeping into your day-to-day activities. Notice whether using the skill provided any rest for your brain. Make a plan to carve out time for rest, including how you'll overcome any resistance to resting.

Creating Positive Moods

Research on positive psychology suggests that creating or focusing on positive emotions can have three important benefits. First, positive emotions help us recover physiologically from stress. Second, they encourage us to engage—to explore, be curious, and take reasonable risks, rather than fighting, fleeing, or freezing. Engaging can lead us to new information and resources that may help us deal with stressors. Third, positive emotions can help us think more broadly about our stressors, which increases our chances of finding novel and creative solutions.

OBSERVE

What's an activity that usually results in positive emotions for you? Consider activities that have one or more of these aspects:

- Play and creativity
- Exploring and trying new things
- Enjoying nature or beauty
- Practicing gratitude
- Recalling positive memories
- Spending time with loved ones
- Sports or entertainment
- Challenging tasks
- Humor (such as jokes and funny shows)

Then make a plan to do it.

What activity will you do?

When will you do it?

REFLECT

Soon after you finish the activity, spend some time writing about the experience. What did it teach you about how you can deal with your stressors?

CHANGE

What kind of "resilience plan" will you build in which you proactively engage in activities that create positive emotions and then deliberately use these positive moods to fuel your thinking about your stressor?

Positive emotions and mental states increase our stress resilience, like sturdy tree branches that bend but don't break when battered by a storm.

Growing Gratitude

When you practice gratitude, you deliberately focus on the good things in your life and feel appreciative. Practicing gratitude can change your perspective on your stressor to a sense of acceptance, openness, and contentment. It can create the broad-minded thinking that helps you view your life and problems from a more optimistic perspective. It counteracts the tendency to overvalue and obsess about the things that are threatened by the stressor. It can also help you overcome a sense of failure or defeat. Gratitude can help protect your relationships from the effects of stress, when you realize how much your loved ones mean to you, and it can motivate you to cope in healthy ways and persist when things get difficult.

OBSERVE

Try a daily gratitude diary for a week. Doing it in the evening is best so you can reflect on what you experienced that day.

When will you write your daily gratitude diary? How will you remind yourself to do it on your set schedule?

REFLECT

Each time you write, reflect on what happened that day and write down as many as five things—large or small—that you feel grateful for. These might be the people you love, your pet, the activities that give your life meaning, people who help you, the abundance of nature, the things that nourish you, or anything else you choose to write about. Try to write about different things rather than repeating the same thought every time. Explain, in just one sentence if you like, what each thing adds to your life.

DAY 1:

1. ____________________
2. ____________________
3. ____________________
4. ____________________
5. ____________________

DAY 2:

1. ____________________
2. ____________________
3. ____________________
4. ____________________
5. ____________________

DAY 3:

1. ____________________
2. ____________________
3. ____________________
4. ____________________
5. ____________________

DAY 4:

1. __________
2. __________
3. __________
4. __________
5. __________

DAY 5:

1. __________
2. __________
3. __________
4. __________
5. __________

DAY 6:

1. __________
2. __________
3. __________
4. __________
5. __________

DAY 7:

1. __________
2. __________
3. __________
4. __________
5. __________

CHANGE

After seven days, record any effects you noticed from your gratitude practice. How might a gratitude practice affect your stress? Is this something you want to continue? If so, how?

Practicing gratitude can help you feel better about your life. It has a kind of grounding effect that gives your prefrontal cortex more power to rein in the wayward amygdala.

Seeing the Benefits of Stress

Whether you think about stress as beneficial or harmful can affect the way you approach the stressor and its ultimate outcome. You can believe that stress will sap your energy and damage your health, or you can believe that stress presents a growth and learning opportunity.

If you see stressful events as meaningful or as manageable personal challenges, you'll feel pride and excitement. Although your body may still go into fight-flight-or-freeze mode, with the same racing heart and sweaty palms, this may feel invigorating rather than overwhelming, like riding a roller coaster or skydiving. And when it's done, you'll feel like a better person for having done the difficult task. You may find you can do something even more difficult the next time. You may start to see yourself as resilient, capable, or even brave.

OBSERVE

How does the concept of embracing stress, rather than trying to reduce it, land with you? What about the idea that stress can be beneficial?

Would any of these thought strategies resonate with you as way ways of embracing your stress? If so, how?

- Focusing on the positive aspects of your body's stress response, such as the extra energy and motivation it gives you
- Viewing yourself as somebody who can successfully cope with stress by adapting and growing with each new experience
- Viewing stress as inevitable and universal; not taking it personally

REFLECT

What do you think of the idea that interpreting your feelings of anxiety as excitement may actually help your mood and performance more than trying to calm down? What would it be like to think of your stressors as challenges rather than threats?

CHANGE

Thinking about a specific stressor you're facing, write your answers to these questions:

Does this stressor provide any opportunities to stretch yourself and learn new skills: for example, work skills, assertiveness skills, communication skills, time management, or self-control? Explain.

Does this stressor have the potential to make you a stronger, wiser, or better person? Describe how this could come about.

Does this stressor provide the opportunity to deepen your relationship(s) in some way, such as by turning to others for help; helping others; working together; becoming a better leader, partner, or parent; or becoming kinder and more empathic? Explain.

How might this stressor help you clarify or change your priorities in life so that you can be happier and healthier? Could this stressor help you grow personally or spiritually? Explain.

Seeing stress as beneficial can help you accept feelings of stress and use the boost of energy they provide to work hard and give it all you've got.

Becoming Gritty

The concept of grit (theorized by psychology professor Angela Duckworth) encompasses the qualities of determination, passion, and purpose. Gritty people are driven to success, have a passion for what they're doing, and are willing to stick it out when things get difficult. Gritty people know their priorities and keep their long-term goals in mind.

Now you might be wondering, *What does grit have to do with stress?* Grit requires using your prefrontal cortex to calm your amygdala, controlling the impulse to run away from a stressful situation or be overwhelmed. It involves deliberately changing your perspective from the short-term stressor to the long-term view.

A gritty mindset helps you act strategically and preserve your energy for the long haul. Gritty people take responsibility for their contribution to problem situations and seek to learn and improve, rather than to avoid stress. They have the vision and confidence that helps them see failure, when it occurs, as an inevitable part of life—not a disaster—and accept and put up with stress in the service of long-term goals.

OBSERVE

Take some time to think about your long-term goals. What do you want to accomplish in the next year? Two years? Five years? Write a one- or two-line summary of your long-term goal(s). For example, "I want to be a successful dentist," "I want to do what I love," "I want to master oil painting,"

"I want to be part of a community," "I want to find a life partner," or "I want to raise confident kids."

REFLECT

Choose one of the goals you listed and answer these questions.

How committed are you to this goal? Why is it so meaningful or personally important to you?

What types of stress or discomfort are you willing to put up with in order to move closer to your goal (for example, failure, rejection, uncertainty, fatigue, and so on)? How will successfully coping with or tolerating your stressors move you closer to this goal?

What can you do to increase your stamina so you can better withstand stress? What might help you feel more sturdy, steady, strong, energized, or optimistic?

CHANGE

How might you reframe the way you think about your stressor so that it feels more like a learning opportunity and less like a permanent obstacle to attaining your life goals?

When you're gritty, your passion for the goal keeps you motivated and lifts your spirits.

You Are the Boss of Your Brain

Congratulations! You made it to the end of the journal. Take a moment to appreciate your effort and dedication to changing your brain to stress less. Through the process of completing this journal, you've gained a greater understanding of your brain's stress response. You've tapped into your own ability to rein in your brain's reactivity to stress so you can thoughtfully respond and recover from stressful situations. You've discovered growth-enhancing aspects of stressful situations for you personally, and you've learned about mindfulness, emotional awareness, self-compassion, perceiving control, and other strategies for calming your amygdala's perception of threat. You've also learned new strategies to help you use your prefrontal cortex and the thinking parts of your brain to manage stress and succeed no matter what life throws at you. You've learned skills to overcome guilt and perfectionism or hypervigilance, break free of thinking traps, practice gratitude, and persist despite obstacles.

In today's rapidly changing world, a stress-resilient brain is the best thing you can have for staying focused, healthy, connected, and on top of your game. It's also true that, even though you've changed your brain to improve your response to stress, stress management is ongoing, and the need for it will naturally ebb and flow in your life.

However, you now have more control over how you react to the stressful situations and circumstances you might encounter. Revisit the tools and prompts in this journal regularly to keep yourself resilient when you're dealing with particularly stressful situations. Return to the prompts you found most helpful and work with them again to generate inner calm and facilitate clear thinking. It'll sustain you for the long haul.

Having a stress-proof brain means being able to slow things down, ground yourself, and overcome feelings of anxiety and helplessness that may have their roots in past difficult experiences. It means being in charge of your own brain, rather than letting your amygdala run the show. Thanks to your commitment in completing this journal, you know how to pivot your thinking from fear and pessimism to openness, hope, curiosity, and creativity. This change in mindset will help you stay healthier, be happier, have better relationships, be successful in business, or be a leader in your company or community. You can't avoid your stressors, but you can learn to see them as challenges that help you grow and become the best version of yourself!

MELANIE GREENBERG, PHD, is a practicing psychologist, author, speaker, and coach in San Diego and throughout California; an expert on managing stress, health, and relationships using proven techniques from neuroscience, mindfulness, and cognitive behavioral therapy (CBT); and author of *The Stress-Proof Brain*. With more than twenty years of experience as a professor, writer, researcher, clinician, and coach, She has delivered workshops and talks to national and international audiences.

Greenberg writes the *Mindful Self-Express* blog for Psychology Today, and is a popular media expert who has been quoted on CNN, Forbes, BBC Radio, ABC News, Yahoo! Shine, and Lifehacker; as well as in *Self*, *Redbook*, *Men's Health*, *Women's Health*, *Fitness*, *Woman's Day*, *Cosmopolitan*, and *HuffPost*. She has also appeared on radio shows like *Leading with Emotional Intelligence*, *The Best People We Know*, *Inner Healers*, and *Winning Life Through Pain*. Greenberg was named one of the thirty most prominent psychologists to follow on Twitter.